SHARE the MUSIC

McGRAW-HILL

AUTHORS

Judy Bond,
Coordinating Author

René Boyer-Alexander

Margaret Campbelle-Holman

Marilyn Copeland Davidson,
Coordinating Author

Robert de Frece

Mary Goetze
Coordinating Author

Doug Goodkin

Betsy M. Henderson

Michael Jothen

Carol King

Vincent P. Lawrence,
Coordinating Author

Nancy L.T. Miller

Ivy Rawlins

Susan Snyder,
Coordinating Author

McGraw-Hill School Division

New York   Farmington

ACKNOWLEDGMENTS

Grateful acknowledgment is given to the following authors, composers, and publishers. Every effort has been made to trace the ownership of all copyrighted material and to secure the necessary permissions to reprint these selections. In the case of some selections for which acknowledgment is not given, extensive research has failed to locate the copyright holders.

Bookstop Literary Agency for *Oranges* from FAMILY PICTURES by Carmen Lomas Garza. Copyright © 1990 by Carmen Lomas Garza. All rights reserved. Used with permission from Children's Book Press through BookStop Literary Agency.

Boosey & Hawkes, Inc. for *Pease Porridge Hot* from LET'S SING TOGETHER for Denise Bacon. Copyright © 1971 by Boosey & Hawkes, Inc. Reprinted by permission.

Margaret Campbelle-Holman for *Kaeru no Uta* and *Kobuta*, collected by Margaret Campbelle-Holman. For *The LaSoMi Bird* by Margaret Campbell-Holman. Copyright © by Margaret Campbelle-Holman.

Randy DeLelles for *Pumpkin Stew* by Randy DeLelles. Copyright © by Randy DeLelles.

E.P.Dutton for *The End* from NOW WE ARE SIX by A.A. Milne. Copyright 1927 by E.P. Dutton, renewed © 1955 by A.A. Milne. Used by permission of Dutton Children's Books, a division of Penguin Books USA Inc.

Farrar, Straus, & Giroux, Inc. for *two friends* from SPIN A SOFT BLACK SONG by Nikki Giovanni. Copyright © 1971, 1985 by Nikki Giovanni. Reprinted by permission of Farrar, Straus & Giroux, Inc.

Barbara M. Hales for *Sidewalk Measles* by Barbara M. Hales. Used by permission of Barbara M. Hales, who holds all copyrights.

Claire Hamil for *The World Is Singing a Song* by Claire Hamil. Copyright © 1998 by Claire Hamil.

Carol Quimby and Sarah Sedgwick Heath for *Chucu* and *Little Tommy Tucker* from THE SONG GARDEN, Book One, published 1984 by The Kodály Musical Training Institute. Copyright © 1984 by Carol Quimby Heath and Sarah Sedgwick Heath.

Holt, Rinehart and Winston Inc. for *Hey, Mr. Monday* (aka *Mr. Monday*) from EXPLORING MUSIC, Grade 1, by Eunice Boardman and Beth Landis. Copyright © 1975 by Holt, Rinehart and Winston, Inc. adapted by permission of the publisher.

The Hokuseido Press for *A flash of lightning!* by Buson. Copyright © 1949, 1981 by R. H. Blyth. Reprinted by permission of the Hokuseido Press, Tokyo, Japan.

Homeland Publishing for *One Light, One Sun*, Words and Music by RAFFI. Copyright © 1985 Homeland Publishing, a division of Troubadour Records. All rights reserved. Used by permission.

Gina Maccoby Literary Agency for *Question* by Mary Ann Hoberman from YELLOW BUTTER, PURPLE JELLY, RED JAM, BLACK BREAD. Reprinted by permission of Gina Maccoby Literary Agency. Copyright © 1981 by Mary Ann Hoberman.

Lillian Moore for *Sometimes* by Lillian Moore. Copyright © by Lillian Moore.

Grace Nash Publications for *Hallowe'en* by Grace Nash. Copyright © 1965, by permission of Grace Nash, author.

Marian Reiner for *Day Music* by Sandra Liatsos. Copyright © 1994 by Sandra Liatsos. Used by permission of Marian Reiner for the author.

Plymouth Music Co. for *Hello Ev'rybody* by Charity Bailey. Copyright by Plymouth Music Co.

Jack Prelutsky for *I Know All the Sounds That the Animals Make* by Jack Prelutsky. Copyright © by Jack Prelutsky.

Silver, Burdett & Ginn Inc. for *In and Out* by Aden G. Lewis. Copyright © 1971 Silver Burdett Company. Used by permission.

Union of American Hebrew Congregations for *Dreidel Song* by Efraim Rosenzweig. Copyright © Union of American Hebrew Congregations.

Continued on page 139

McGraw-Hill School Division
A Division of The McGraw-Hill Companies

McGraw-Hill School Division
Two Penn Plaza
New York, NY 10121

Printed in the United States of America
ISBN 0-02-295052-4 / 1
1 2 3 4 5 6 7 8 9 004 04 03 02 01 00 99

Special Contributors

Contributing Writer
Janet McMillion

Consultant Writers
Teri Burdette, Signing
Brian Burnett, Movement
Robert Duke, Assessment
Joan Gregoryk, Vocal Development/
  Choral
Judith Jellison, Special Learners/
  Assessment
Jacque Schrader, Movement
Kathy B. Sorensen, International Phonetic
  Alphabet
Mollie Tower, Listening

Consultants
Lisa DeLorenzo, Critical Thinking
Nancy Ferguson, Jazz/Improvisation
Judith Nayer, Poetry
Marta Sanchez, Dalcroze
Mollie Tower, Reviewer
Robyn Turner, Fine Arts

Multicultural Consultants
Judith Cook Tucker
JaFran Jones
Oscar Muñoz
Marta Sanchez
Edwin J. Schupman, Jr., of ORBIS
  Associates
Mary Shamrock
Kathy B. Sorensen

Multicultural Advisors
Shailaja Akkapeddi (Hindi), Edna Alba
(Ladino), Gregory Amobi (Ibu), Thomas
Appiah (Ga, Twi, Fanti), Deven Asay
(Russian), Vera Auman (Russian, Ukrainian),
David Azman (Hebrew), Lissa Bangeter
(Portuguese), Britt Marie Barnes (Swedish),
Dr. Mark Bell (French), Brad Ahawanrathe
Bonaparte (Mohawk), Chhanda Chakroborti
(Hindi), Ninthalangsonk Chanthasen
(Laotian), Julius Chavez (Navajo), Lin-Rong
Chen (Mandarin), Anna Cheng (Mandarin),
Rushen Chi (Mandarin), T. L. Chi (Mandarin),
Michelle Chingwa (Ottowa), Hoon Choi
(Korean), James Comarell (Greek), Lynn
DePaula (Portuguese), Ketan Dholakia
(Gujarati), Richard O. Effiong (Nigerian),
Nayereh Fallahi (Persian), Angela Fields
(Hopi, Chemehuevi), Gary Fields (Lakota,

Cree), Siri Veslemoy Fluge (Norwegian),
Katalin Forrai (Hungarian), Renee Galagos
(Swedish), Linda Goodman, Judith A. Gray,
Savyasachi Gupta (Marati), Elizabeth Haile
(Shinnecock), Mary Harouny (Persian),
Charlotte Heth (Cherokee), Tim Hunt
(Vietnamese), Marcela Janko (Czech), Raili
Jeffrey (Finnish), Rita Jensen (Danish), Teddy
Kaiahura (Swahili), Gueen Kalaw (Tagalog),
Merehau Kamai (Tahitian), Richard Keeling,
Masanori Kimura (Japanese), Chikahide
Komura (Japanese), Saul Korewa (Hebrew),
Jagadishwar Kota (Tamil), Sokun Koy
(Cambodian), Craig Kurumada (Balkan),
Cindy Trong Le (Vietnamese), Dongchoon Lee
(Korean), Young-Jing Lee (Korean), Nomi Lob
(Hebrew), Sam Loeng (Mandarin, Malay),
Georgia Magpie (Comanche), Mladen Marič
(Croatian), Kuinise Matagi (Samoan), Hiromi
Matsushita (Japanese), Jackie Maynard
(Hawaiian), David McAllester, Mike
Kanathohare McDonald (Mohawk),
Khumbulani Mdlefshe (Zulu), Martin Mkize
(Xhosa), David Montgomery (Turkish), Kazadi
Big Musungayi (Swahili), Professor Akiya
Nakamara (Japanese), Edwin Napia (Maori),
Hang Nguyen (Vietnamese), Richard Nielsen
(Danish), Wil Numkena (Hopi), Eva Ochoa
(Spanish), Drora Oren (Hebrew), Jackie
Osherow (Yiddish), Mavis Oswald (Russian),
Dr. Dil Parkinson (Arabic), Kenny Tahawisoren
Perkins (Mohawk), Alvin Petersen (Sotho),
Phay Phan (Cambodian), Charlie Phim
(Cambodian), Aroha Price (Maori), Marg Puiri
(Samoan), John Rainer (Taos Pueblo, Creek),
Lillian Rainer (Taos Pueblo, Creek, Apache),
Winton Ria (Maori), Arnold Richardson
(Haliwa-Saponi), Thea Roscher (German),
Dr. Wayne Sabey (Japanese), Regine Saintil
(Bamboula Creole), Luci Scherzer (German),
Ken Sekaquaptewa (Hopi), Samouen Seng
(Cambodian), Pei Shin (Mandarin), Dr. Larry
Shumway (Japanese), Gwen Shunatona
(Pawnee, Otoe, Potawatomi), Ernest Siva
(Cahuilla, Serrano [Maringa´]), Ben Snowball
(Inuit), Dr. Michelle Stott (German), Keiko
Tanefuji (Japanese), James Taylor
(Portuguese), Shiu-wai Tong (Mandarin),
Tom Toronto (Lao, Thai), Lynn Tran
(Vietnamese), Gulavadee Vaz (Thai), Chen
Ying Wang (Taiwanese), Masakazu Watabe
(Japanese), Freddy Wheeler (Navajo), Keith
Yackeyonny (Comanche), Liming Yang
(Mandarin), Edgar Zurita (Andean)

CONTENTS

The World is Singing a Song

Waves splash
Raindrops drum

  The world is singing a song.

Thunders crash
Winds hum

  The world is singing a song.

Icicles snap
Fires fizzle

  The world is bringing a song.

Lakes lap
Deserts sizzle

  The world is singing a song.

  It sings for me!

—Claire Hamil

1

HELLO EVERYONE!

Hello

Words and Music by Teresa Jennings

Meet the Beat

LISTENING

Music from Bali
Gamelan Ensemble

Listen for the **steady beat**.

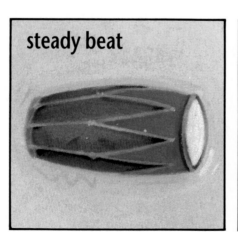

steady beat

steady beat

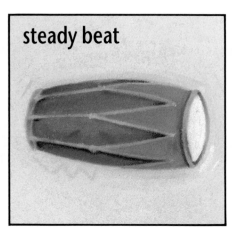

steady beat

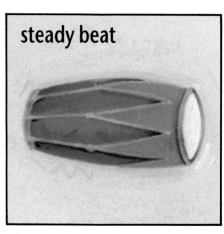

Loud Sounds, Soft Sounds

Which things make **loud** sounds?
Which things make **soft** sounds?

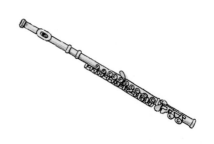

loud

soft

What do you hear?

loud

loud

loud

soft

soft

loud

soft

soft

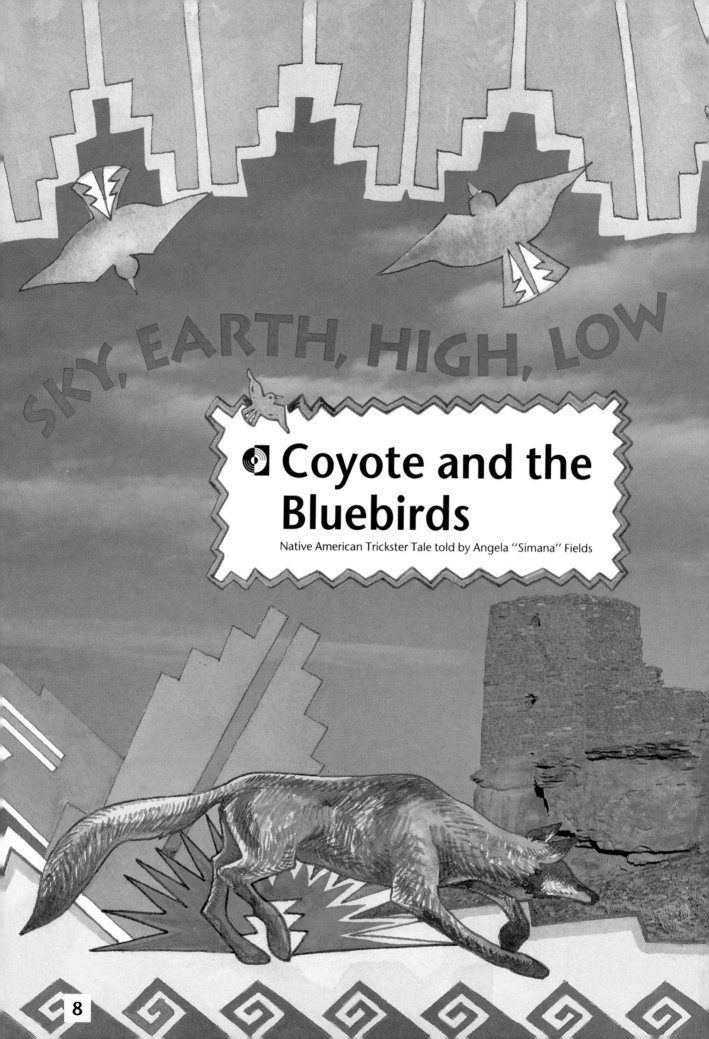

Coyote and the Bluebirds

Native American Trickster Tale told by Angela "Simana" Fields

The bluebirds fly **high.**

Coyote walks **low.**

Music can sound **high** and **low.**

Move to the Music

🎵 Hungarian Dance

LISTENING

No. 6

by Johannes Brahms

The dancers' steps may be
slow or **fast.**

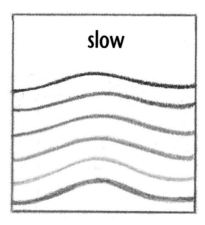

slow

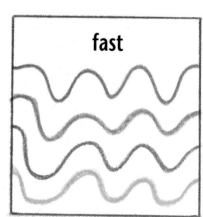

fast

10

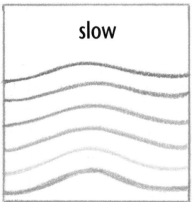

slow

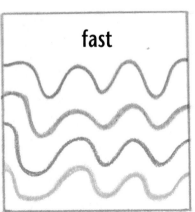

fast

Picture a SOUND

The painting shows a happy time.

What sounds do you hear when you look at it?

The artist is Carmen Lomas Garza.

Long and Short, High and Low

Croak

squeak

honk

Mooooooooo

Hoot Hoot

Oink Oink

14

I Know All the Sounds that the Animals Make

I know all the sounds that the animals make,
and make them all day from the moment I wake,
I roar like a mouse and I purr like a moose,
I hoot like a duck and I moo like a goose.

I squeak like a cat and I quack like a frog,
I oink like a bear and I honk like a hog,
I croak like a cow and I bark like a bee,
no wonder the animals marvel at me.

—*Jack Prelutsky*

Reach Up Bend Down

LISTENING

Of a Tailor and a Bear
by Edward MacDowell

The tailor sews a suit. Then a special visitor comes.

①

②

LISTEN
TO MY VOICE

This is my speaking voice.

This is my whispering voice.

This is my singing voice.

This is my
calling voice.

LONG
and
SHORT

Find things here that are long and short.

Make sounds that are long and short.

HIGH
AND LOW

Wishy Washy

English Singing Game

Find the tuba and the piccolo.

Which one makes high sounds?
Which one makes low sounds?

Music is written on a staff. A **staff** has five lines and four spaces.

Music Moves Me

Music can make you move in different ways.

Fly with the Bees

Honeybees get nectar from flowers.
They make nectar into honey.

How does a bee move?

What sound does it make?

Flight of the Bumblebee

by Nikolai Rimsky-Korsakov

Sound and move like a bee. This music will help you.

Flight '76

by Walter Murphy

Make up your own bee dance.

Tapping, Walking, Dancing

Sometimes

Sometimes
   When I skip or hop
   or when I'm
      jumping
Suddenly
   I like to stop
   and listen to me
      thumping.

—*Lillian Moore*

Cobbler, Cobbler

English Nursery Rhyme

Cob - bler, cob - bler, mend my shoe.

Get it done by half past two.

30

Cob - bler,   cob - bler,   mend my   shoe.

Get   it   done by   half   past   two.

Why are there two shoes
above "cobbler"?
Why is there one shoe
above "shoe"?

Go Slow, Go Fast

The Story of Epaminondas

Hispanic and African American Folk Tale

and

top

tip

very

the

to

up

up

up

up

. . . up

Read the words.

Get slower as you go up the hill.
Get faster as you come down.

down

down

down

down

down
he
came
and then he stopped.

You Can Read Rhythm!

Say "shoe" for ♩

Say "cobbler" for ♫

Cobbler, Cobbler

English Nursery Rhyme

Cob - bler,   cob - bler,   mend my   shoe.

Get   it   done by   half past   two.

Say "gate" for ♩

Say "garden" for ♫

🎵 Two, Four, Six, Eight

English Nursery Rhyme

Two, four, six, eight,

Meet me at the gar - den gate.

If I'm late, don't wait.

Two, four, six, eight.

Faster and Slower

🔊 Little Red Caboose

American Children's Song

When does the train **get faster?**
When does the train **get slower?**

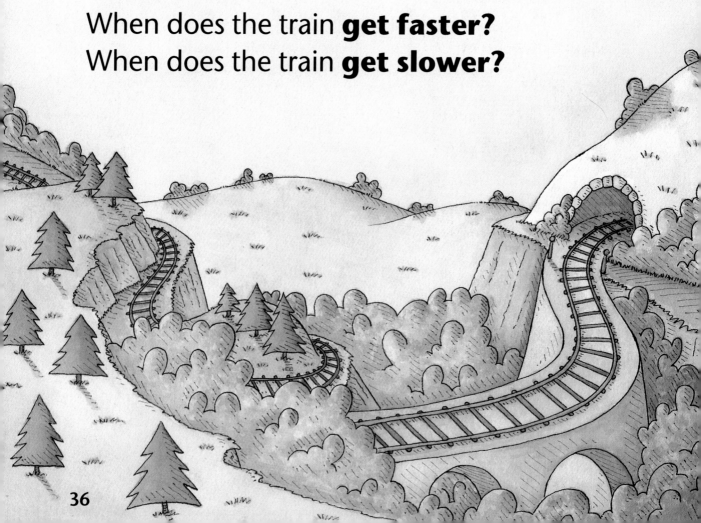

Little red caboose, little red caboose,
Little red caboose behind the train, the train.
Smokestack on its back, going down the track,
Little red caboose behind the train.

DANCE
with the
BEAT

LISTENING

Little Bird Dance
Traditional Dance

Dance faster when the beat gets faster.

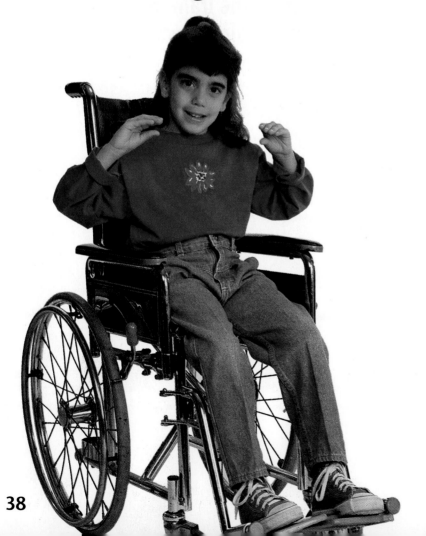

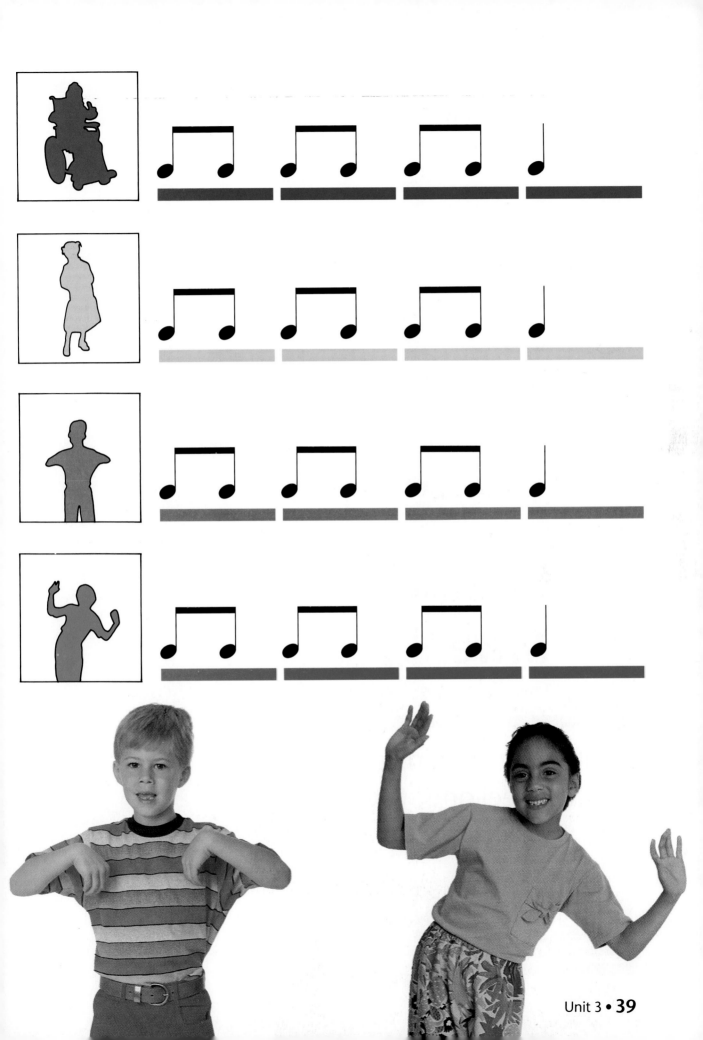

Beats in Twos

Mwe

Tanzanian Counting Song

Beats can move in sets of two.
You can feel one **strong beat** and
one **weak beat**.

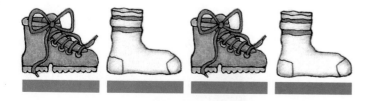

and Threes

Waltz No. 3
by Amy Marcy Beach

Beats can move in sets of three.
You can feel one **strong beat**
and two **weak beats.**

ANIMAL FUN

LISTENING

The Carnival of the Animals

by Camille Saint-Saëns

Imagine music about each animal.
Every piece would sound different.
Which animals do you hear?

SUNNY DAYS

Sidewalk Measles

I saw the sidewalk catch measles
When the rain came down today.
It started with a little blotching—
Quickly spread to heavy splotching,
Then as I continued watching
The rain-rash slowly dried away.

—*Barbara M. Hales*

Falling Rain

You can listen to music on a rainy day.

C-A-G
by Billy Taylor

Let your hands show higher and lower.

The raindrops show how the melody goes.

🔊 Rain, Rain, Go Away

Traditional Children's Song

Rain,

rain,

go a-

way

Make Rain Sounds

Make the sound of
raindrops on **woods.**

Make the sound of
thunder on **drums.**

A flash of lightning!
The sound of dew
dripping down the bamboos.
—*Buson*

Name the Pitches

High and low pitches are on the staff.
If *so* is in a space, *mi* is in the space below.

so   mi

Rain, rain, go a - way.

If *so* is around a line, where is *mi*?

Tinker, Tailor

English Button-Counting Game

so

Tin - ker,   tai - lor,   sol - dier,   sail - or,

rich man,   poor man,   beg-gar man,   thief.

What Will You Play?

Play more drums and woods with "A Flash of Lightning."

◀ Weave Me the Sunshine

Play **scrapers** and **shakers**.

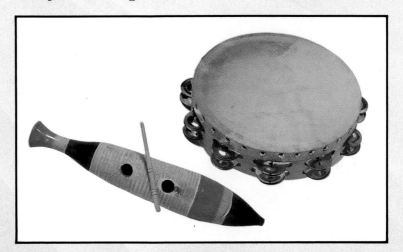

◀ Umi wa Hiroi na
Big Ocean

Play **metal** instruments.

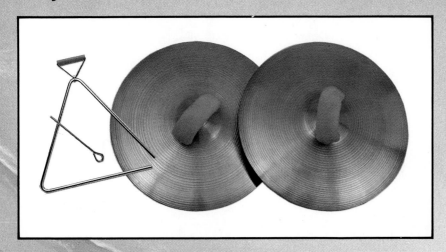

You can sing!
Whales can sing too!

Follow the lines.

Make your voice go up and down.

Which sounds do the whales make?

And God Created Great Whales

by Alan Hovhaness

Listen to the orchestra.

How can their music sound like whales?

Sing, Speak, Create

When will you use your speaking voice?

Two, Four, Six, Eight

English Nursery Rhyme
Music by Marilyn Davidson

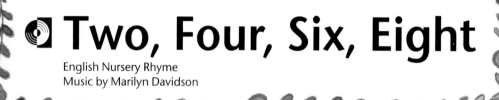

Two, four, six, eight,

Meet me at the gar-den gate.

If I'm late, don't wait.

Two, four, six, eight.

Make up a melody for Line 3.

It can go

up

or down.

It can stay the same, like this

or stay the same, like this.

Now sing the new song.

The Music is You!

Meet  Gregory Hines

Gregory Hines makes music.
He uses his voice and
his body.

You can make music too.
Sing, speak, call,
or whisper.
Make sounds with
your hands and feet.

Move your body to show how
music sounds.

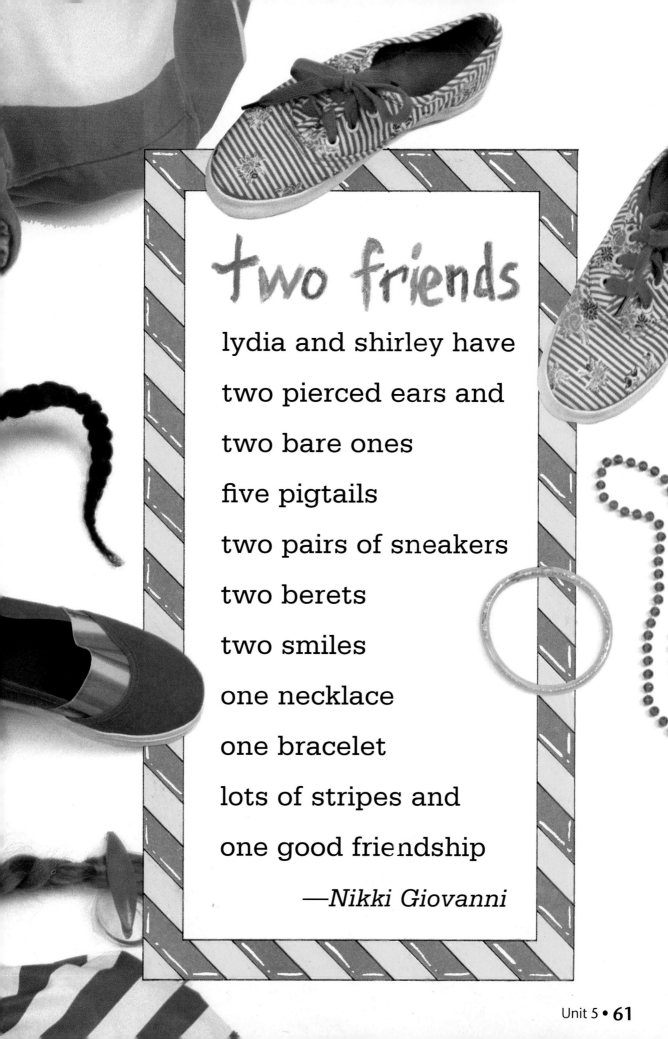

two friends

lydia and shirley have

two pierced ears and

two bare ones

five pigtails

two pairs of sneakers

two berets

two smiles

one necklace

one bracelet

lots of stripes and

one good friendship

—Nikki Giovanni

SOUND
No Sound

Point to the beat bars.

Tap once for each boat.

Which beat has no sound?

Which beat has two sounds?

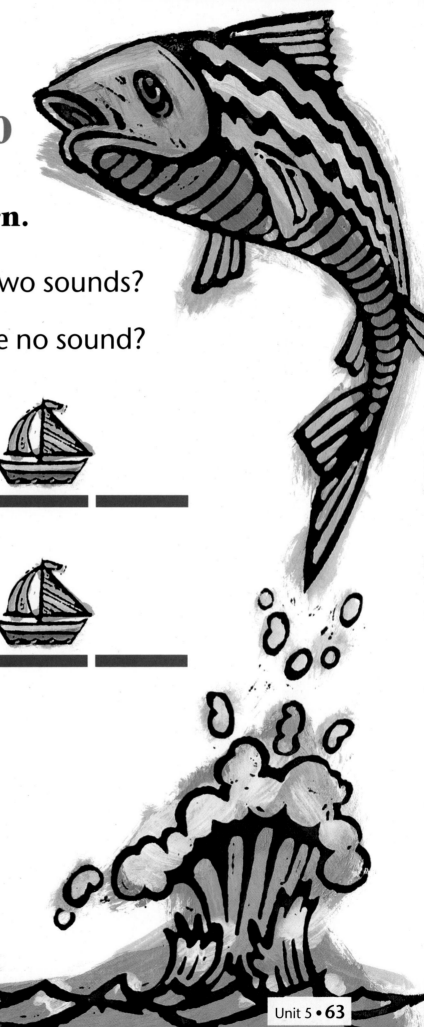

El barquito

Panamanian Folk Song

Tap the pattern.

Which beat has two sounds?

Which beats have no sound?

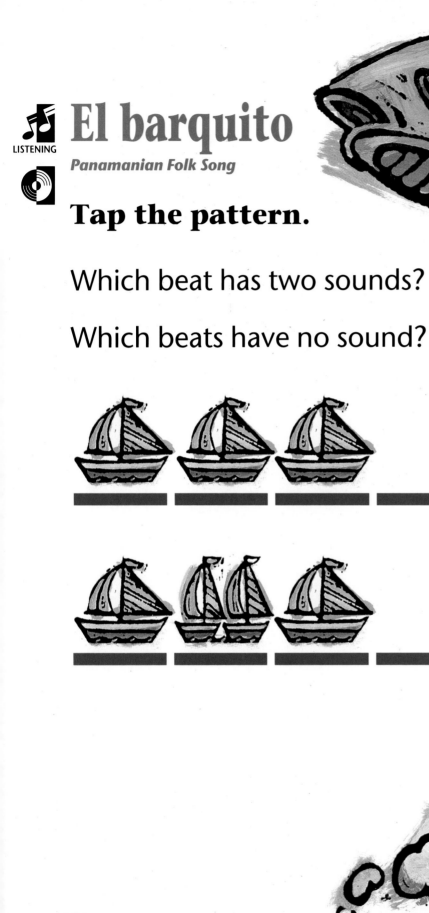

Wavy Crackers

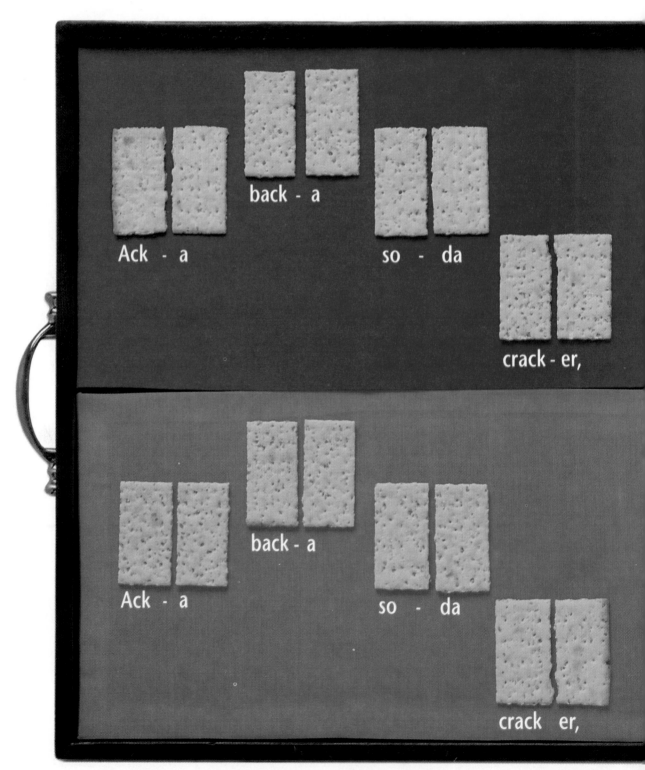

back - a

Ack - a   so - da

crack - er,

back - a

Ack - a   so - da

crack   er,

Acka Backa
Playground Game

The crackers show the melody.

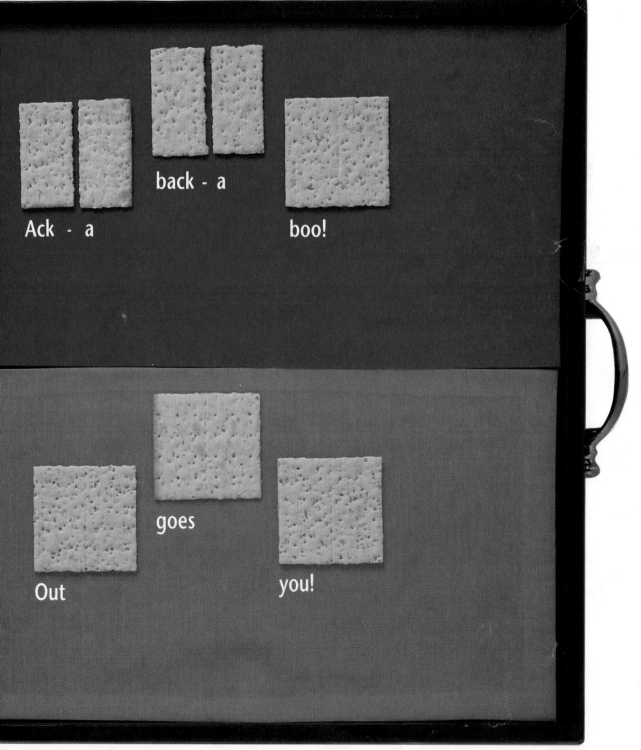

Sign for Silence

Bu-bu-bu

Piglet
こ ぶ た
ko bu ta

Pon-poko-pon

Raccoon
た ぬ き
ta nu ki

Kon-kon-kon

Fox
き つ ね
ki tsu ne

Nya-o

Cat
ね こ
ne ko

Kobuta

Japanese Children's Song

When do you sing?
When are you silent?

ko bu ta

ta nu ki

ki tsu ne

ne ko

The sign for no sound on a beat is 𝄽

It is called a rest.

Say "bowl" for ♩

Say "jelly" for ♫

Move your hands apart for 𝄽

Jelly in the Bowl

American Rhyme

A Song with 3 Pitches

You have sung songs with *mi* and *so*.
Now sing a song with another pitch.

so   ?   so   mi

We Are Playing in the Forest

American Singing Game

We are play-ing in the for-est

for the wolf is far a-way.

Who knows what will hap-pen to us

if he finds us at our play?

Free to Sing

The LaSoMi Bird

by Margaret Campbelle-duGard

Listen and follow the pictures.

Meeshon and the bird sing:

la so mi   la so mi

Match each rhythm with a clock you hear.

QUESTION?

The grownups say I'm growing tall
And that my clothes are growing small.
Can clothes grow *small*?
I always think
That things grow *big*
Or else they shrink.
But did they shrink
Or did I grow
Or did we both change?
I don't know.

—**Mary Ann Hoberman**

Sam
Age 4

A song grows when a section
is added.

The first section is called A.

The second section is called B.

LISTENING

La raspa

Mexican Folk Music

Play instruments with the beat.

One Sound, Two Sounds, No Sound

| Old | man | Old | wom - an | Grand - daugh-ter |

The Great Big Enormous Turnip

Once upon a time an old man
Planted a little turnip.
The turnip grew too big to pull up.
The old man called for help.
Everyone pulled and pulled,
And up came the turnip at last.

—Alexei Tolstoy

Big black dog

Cat

Might-y lit - tle mouse

Say "Hey" for ♩

Say "Mister" for ♫

Here is a song that has this rhythm.

Hey, Mr. Monday

Words and Music by Barbara Andress
Adapted by Sue Snyder

Hey, Mis-ter Mon-day, Play a song, play a song.

Hey, Mis-ter Mon-day, Play a song for me.

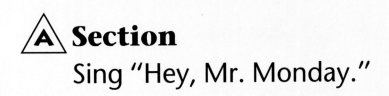

Use what you know to make an AB piece.

⚠ Section

Sing "Hey, Mr. Monday."

Ⓑ Section

Take turns tapping rhythms that last four beats.

Upward and Downward

Pitches get higher as they move **upward.**
Pitches get lower as they move **downward.**

upward ⟶   ⟵ downward

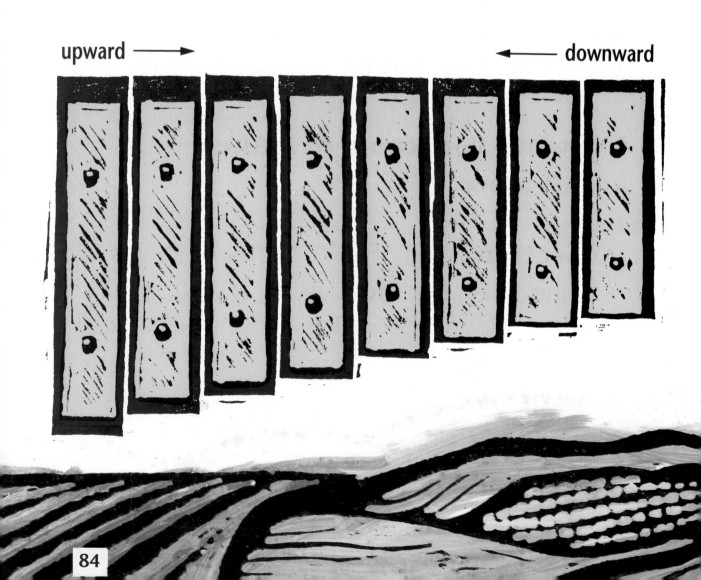

"The Mill Song" has three pitches
you know.

mi so la

The Mill Song

American Singing School Song

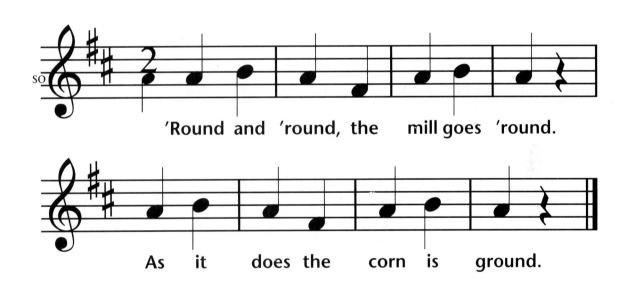

'Round and 'round, the mill goes 'round.

As it does the corn is ground.

◖ One Light, One Sun

Words and Music by Raffi

1. One light, one sun,
   One sun lighting ev'ryone.
   One world turning
   One world turning ev'ryone.

2. One world, one home,
   One world home for ev'ryone.
   One dream, one song,
   One song heard by ev'ryone.

3. One love, one heart,
   One heart warming ev'ryone.
   One hope, one joy,
   One love filling ev'ryone.

   One light, one sun,
   One sun lighting ev'ryone
   One light warming ev'ryone.

ENCORE

THREE
FRIENDS

LISTENING

Fish and Chips
Sung by Sharon, Lois & Bram

Sharon, Lois, and Bram
are a kind of family.
These three people
sing together. This
song is like their
family. It has three
parts, too.

MEET *Sharon, Lois, and Bram*

Listen to Sharon, Lois, and Bram.
They tell about sharing their music
with others.
Other people share music with
them, too.

Who can share their songs with you?

Who might like to hear your songs?

Celebrations

DAY MUSIC

Every day is happy.
Every day is fair.
Every day's a dancing day
When music's in the air.

—*Sandra Liatsos*

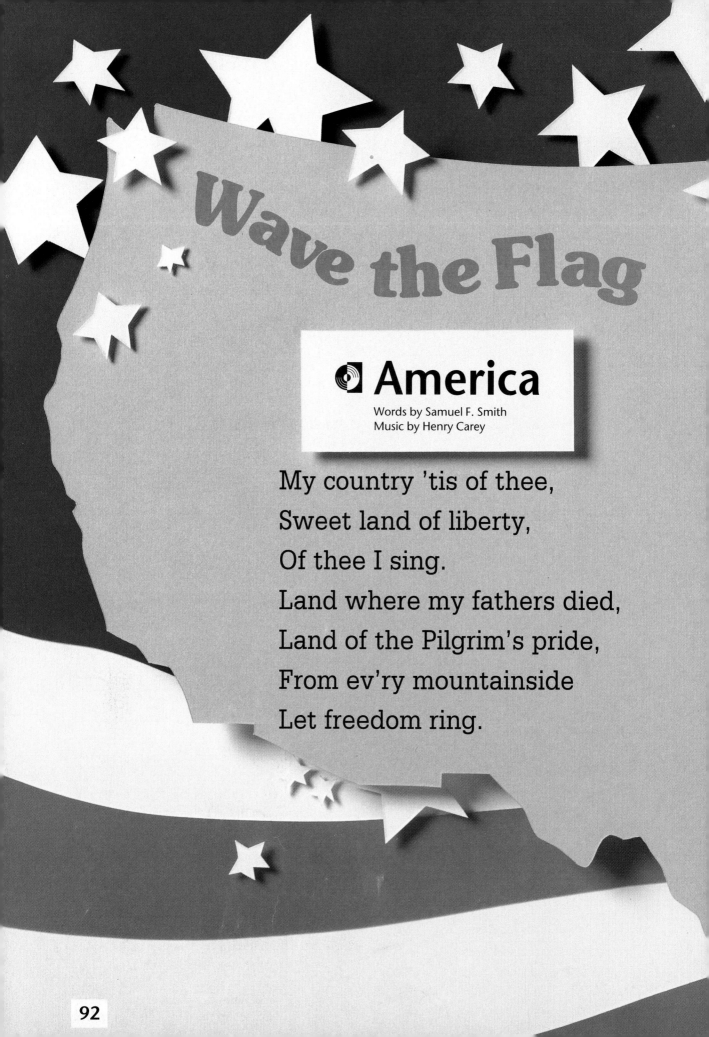

Wave the Flag

America

Words by Samuel F. Smith
Music by Henry Carey

My country 'tis of thee,
Sweet land of liberty,
Of thee I sing.
Land where my fathers died,
Land of the Pilgrim's pride,
From ev'ry mountainside
Let freedom ring.

LISTENING

You're a
Grand Old Flag

Words and Music by George M. Cohan

Pat with the steady beat.
March to it.

Birthday Songs

LISTENING

Listen to people singing birthday songs. The songs are from many countries.

The End

When I was One,
I had just begun.

When I was Two,
I was nearly new.

When I was Three,
I was hardly Me.

When I was Four,
I was not much more.

When I was Five,
I was just alive.

But now I am Six, I'm as clever as clever.
So I think I'll be six now, for ever and ever.
—A. A. Milne

PUT ON A MASK

Halloween is time for pumpkins and dressing up.

Pumpkin Stew

Music by Randy DeLelles   Words by Sue Snyder

Pump-kin stew,   Pump-kin stew,

What shall we put   in the   pump-kin stew?

 **LISTENING** ## Funeral March of a Marionette
by Charles Gounod

Pretend you are dressing up for Halloween.

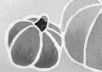

Hallowe'en

Words and Music by Grace C. Nash

Hal-low-e'en, Hal-low-e'en, Pump-kins fat.

Hal-low-e'en, Hal-low-e'en, Pump-kins fat.

Witch-es ride on broom-sticks, Wear-ing sau-cy hats,

Hal-low-e'en, Hal-low-e'en, Big black cats!

Time for Thanks

Clap when you see hands.

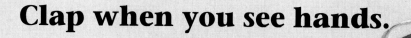

Five Fat Turkeys

American Rhyme

Five fat turkeys are we,

We slept all night in a tree.

When the cook came around we couldn't be found,

So that's why we're here you see.

🎵 Pumpkin Song

Music by Doug Goodkin
American Rhyme

A pumpkin ran away

Before Thanksgiving Day.

Said he, "They'll make a pie out of me

if I should stay."

Days of Snow

What do you see when
the snow falls?
What do you hear?

LISTENING

December Snow
by R. Carlos Nakai

Listen to this music.
It is played on a wood flute.
Why does it sound like falling
snow?

The Woodgatherer

Oscar Howe painted this picture.
He was from South Dakota. Winters
are cold there. Why is this person
gathering wood?

SPIN A TOP

A *dreidel* is a top.
Children play a game with
dreidels at Hanukkah.

Dreidel Song

Twirl about, dance about,
Spin, spin, spin!
Turn, Dreidel, Turn—
Time to begin!

Soon it is Hanukkah—
Fast, Dreidel, fast!
For you will lie still
When Hanukkah's past.
—*Efraim Rosenzweig*

Sing and dance for Hanukkah!

Light the Candles

Words and Music by
Samuel Roeman

Here Comes Santa

LISTENING

March of the Toys

from *Babes in Toyland*
by Victor Herbert

You will hear music
for a parade of toys.
What toys might be
marching?

Tap with the steady beat.

Santa's Helpers

American Song

Sing Joy

O Come Little Children

German Carol

Christmas is about a baby.
Visitors came to see the baby.

🔊 The Friendly Beasts

Traditional English Carol

How do the animals help the baby?

KWANZAA DAYS

Kwanzaa is a holiday that lasts for seven days. Families and friends have a feast on the last day. They sing and dance.

 **Miwɔe Nenyo**

LISTENING

Ewe Folk Song

 This music is from Africa.

People make gifts for Kwanzaa.
The gifts may be beads, clothes,
toys, or pictures.

Hand in Hand

Dr. Martin Luther King, Jr., wanted fairness for all people. What rules help you to be fair and kind?

🔊 Sing About Martin

Words and Music by
"Miss Jackie" Weisman

1. Sing

2. Martin (M)

3. Caring

4. Peace

5. All around the world

Be Mine

We give valentines to special friends.
Think of ways to give valentines.

I Made a Valentine

Words and Music by Lynn Freeman Olson

A-Tisket A-Tasket

Sung by Ella Fitzgerald

LISTENING

Ella Fitzgerald is famous.
She sings jazz.
How does she deliver her letter
in this song?

Signs of Spring

What signs of spring can you find?

Spring Is Coming

Music by Milton Kaye
American Rhyme

**Spring is coming,
Spring is coming,
How do you think I know?
I found some pussy willows.
I know it must be so.**

"Spring"

LISTENING

from **The Four Seasons**, *First Movement*
by Antonio Vivaldi

**Listen to this music
about spring.**

Kaeru no Uta
Frog's Song

Japanese Folk Song
English Version by MMH

Japanese: かえるの うたが
English: Hear the frog, he sings a song.

きこえて くるよ
It is such a hap-py song:

グワ グワ グワ グワ
gwa gwa gwa gwa

ゲロ ゲ ロ ゲ ロ ゲ ロ グワ グワ グワ
ge ro ge ro ge ro ge ro gwa gwa gwa.

More Songs to Read

Steady Beat

Pat the beat like this as you sing.

Beat and No Beat

Which picture shows a steady beat?

High or Low?

**Listen to each animal sound.
Which animal sounds high?
Low? High and low?**

El perrito
(dog)

El gatito
(cat)

El burrito
(donkey)

El patito
(duck)

El chanchito
(pig)

One and Two Sounds to the Beat

Flash your hands like stars to show the rhythm.

Star Light, Star Bright

Fast and Slow

Ride a roller coaster up and down
a hill. When will it go fast?

Roller Coaster Song

Slowly moves the roller coaster
As it climbs the big, high hill.
When it gets up to the top,
(Fast!)
Down it goes. It cannot stop!

Reading Rhythm

Read this rhythm.

Find it in "Los Pollitos."

Loud and Soft Rhythms

Follow a leader and play loud
and soft.

Loud

Soft

LOOSE TOOTH

Anonymous

I had a loose tooth, a wig-gly, jig-gly
loose tooth, I had a loose tooth,
hang-ing by a thread. So I pulled my
loose tooth, this wig-gly, jig-gly loose tooth, And
put it 'neath my pil-low, and then I went to
bed. The fair-ies took my loose tooth, my
wig-gly, jig-gly loose tooth, So now I have a
quar-ter and a hole in my head.

Reading *So* and *Mi*

On which space is *so*? *Mi*?

so   *mi*   *mi*

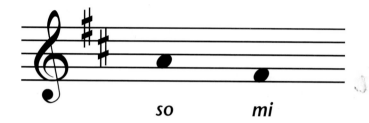

American Song

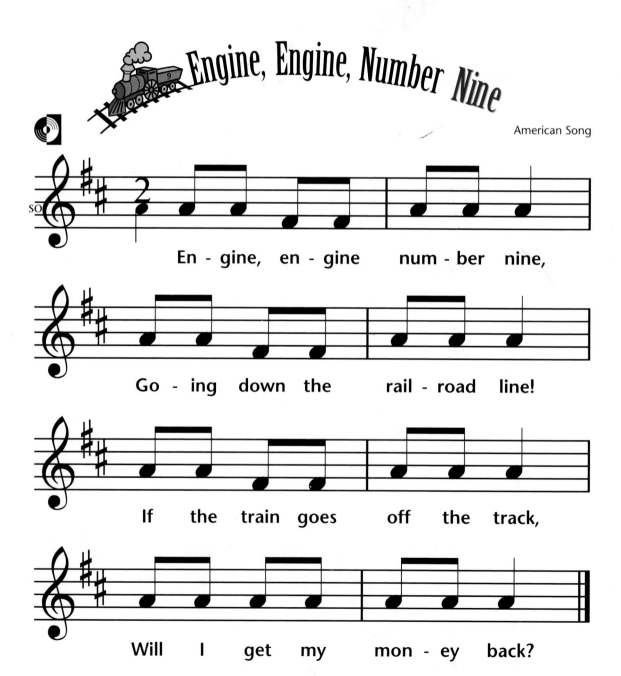

En - gine, en - gine   num - ber nine,

Go - ing   down   the   rail - road   line!

If   the   train goes   off   the   track,

Will   I   get   my   mon - ey   back?

124

So and Mi Around Lines

Around which line is *so*? *Mi*?

Bye, Bye, Baby-O

American Song

Bye, bye, ba - by - O,

Off to dream-land you must go.

SEE SAW

American Song

See - saw up and down,

In the air and on the ground.

Measures

A **staff** shows higher and lower pitches.

staff

Bar lines show **measures**.

bar line   bar line   bar line   bar line   bar line

measure   measure   measure   measure

Quaker, Quaker

American Folk Song

"Quak - er, Quak - er, how is thee?"

"Ver - y well, I thank thee."

"How's thy neigh - bor next to thee?"

"I don't know, I'll go and see."

Chucu

American Song
English Version by MMH

Spanish: Chu - cu, chu - cu, chu - cu cha,
English: Chu - cu, chu - cu, chu - cu cha,

¿Cuán - tas co - sas tra - e - rá?
How much are you car - ry - ing?

Beats in Sets of Two

All beats are not the same.
The strong beat is the first
beat in every measure.

strong   weak   strong   weak

These beats are in sets of two.

2 = the number of beats in a measure

♩ = 1 beat

No Sound on a Beat

Find beats with no sound.

What's your name?   Pud - ding   Tame.

Ask   me a - gain and I'll   tell   you the   same.

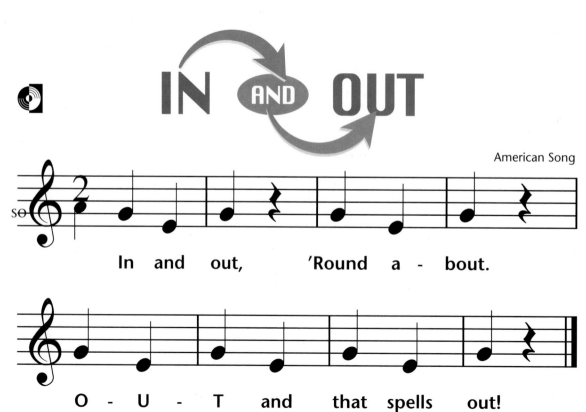

In   and   out,   'Round   a - bout.

O - U - T   and   that   spells   out!

Upward and Downward

Listen for sounds that move upward and sounds that move downward.

LUCY LOCKET

American Song

Lu - cy Lock - et lost her pock - et,

Kit - ty Fish - er found it.

Not a pen - ny was there in it,

On - ly rib - bon 'round it.

The Quarter Rest

The sign for no sound on a beat is
a **quarter rest** (𝄽).

Find the quarter rests.

Pease Porridge Hot

English Nursery Rhyme

1. Pease por - ridge hot,
2. Some like it hot.

Pease por - ridge cold,
Some like it cold.

Pease por - ridge in the pot
Some like it in the pot

Nine days old.

A New Pitch

There is a pitch in "Lucy Locket" that is not *so* or *mi*.

so so ? ? so so mi mi

Is the new pitch higher or lower than *so*?

Singing with *La*

Find *la* in this song.

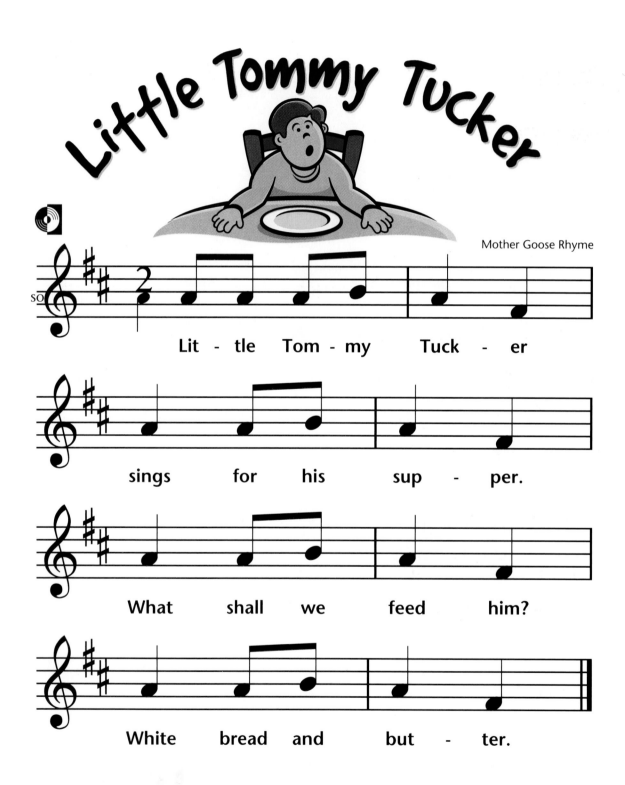

Mother Goose Rhyme

Lit - tle Tom - my Tuck - er

sings for his sup - per.

What shall we feed him?

White bread and but - ter.

132

Singing in AB Form

Music with two different parts is called AB form. These letters can stand for different parts.

Learn a new B part.

I'll sing for my supper,
just like Tommy Tucker.
But I need to say that I don't
care for bread and butter!
I'll sing for my supper,
just like Tommy Tucker.
But I need to say that I would
like some bread and butter!

Use What You Know

Read rhythms and pitches to learn
this song. Then play the game!

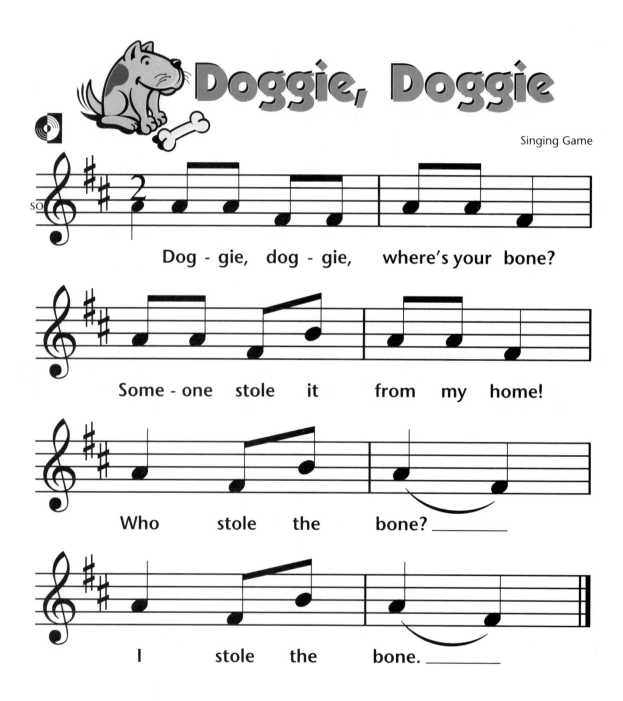

Doggie, Doggie

Singing Game

Dog - gie, dog - gie, where's your bone?

Some - one stole it from my home!

Who stole the bone? _____

I stole the bone. _____

One More Song

Sing this song using *so mi la so*. Make up a B part about friends you want to see!

Good Night, Sleep Tight

Traditional

so

Good   night,   sleep   tight,

Friends will come to - mor - row night.

You're Invited:
Orchestra Concert

Listen, look, and learn!

Use your good manners so everyone can enjoy the music.

This is the orchestra.

Tubby the Tuba

by George Kleinsinger

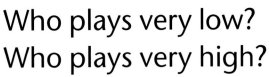

Who plays very low?
Who plays very high?

Talk about the concert.
Share the story of "Tubby the Tuba."

Meet Sam Wong

Sam Wong first played the tuba in the fourth grade.
Now he conducts orchestras.

INDEX OF LITERATURE

INDEX OF LISTENING SELECTIONS

INDEX OF SONGS AND SPEECH PIECES

ART & PHOTO CREDITS

COVER DESIGN: Robert Brook Allen, A Man and His Dog

COVER PHOTOGRAPHY: All photographs are by the McGraw–Hill School Division except as noted below.

ILLUSTRATION

Elizabeth Allen, 8–9, 90–91; Lisa Berrett, 70–71; Joe Boddy, 42–43; Robert Collier Morales, 10–11; Margaret Cusak, 16–17; Don Daily, 114; Darius Detweiler, 68–69, 74–75; Gershom Griffith, 108–109; Patrick Girouard, 22–23; Jean Hiroshima, 52–53, 115; Dennis Hockerman, 0–1, 120,121; John Jones, 76–77; Dave Joly, 58–59; Manuel King, 36–37; Kingta Kung, 62–63; Mike Lacopa, 8–9; Claude Martinot, 34–35; Diana Magnuson, 106–107; Benton Mahon, 28–29; David Milgrim, 94–95; Mas Miyamoto, 66–67; Leo Monahan, 78–79; Gavin Owen, 54–55; Cyndy Patrick, 56–57, 96–97; Kathy Petrauskas, Yuri Salzman, 6–7, 37, 70, 114–115, 116, 117, 118, 122, 127, 135; 4–5; Bob Shein, 92–93; Neil Shigley, 84–85; Patrick Soper, 100–101; Susan Spellman, 72–73; Geraldo Suzan, 86–87; Andrea Z. Tachiera, 123; Peggy Tagel, 104–105; Mary K. Thelen, 18–19; Stan Tusan, 80–83; Rosario Valderania, 32–33; Cornelius Van Wright, 111; Randy Verougstraete, 136–137; Carolyn Vibbert, 12–13; David Wenzel, Kathy Wilburn, 14–15; 30–31; Fred Winkowsky, 98–99; Lane Yerkes, 20–21, 44–45.

PHOTOGRAPHY

All photographs are by the McGraw–Hill School Division (MHSD) except as noted below.

i. r. © Artville. iv. drum, maracas, trumpet, violin, © Artville. v: tambourine, © Artville. **Unit 1** 5: E.R. Degginger/Photo Reseachers, Inc. 8–9: Tom Bean/Stock Market. 11: Joice Veselka. 13: *Oranges* by Carmen Lomas Barza from book "Family Pictures," photo/Bill Walzer for MHSD. **Unit 2** 18, 19: Bill Walzter for MHSD.

24: b.r. Janet Century; l. Tom McCarthy; t.r. Betts Anderson/Unicord Stock Photo. 25: b. Daniele Pellegrini/Photo Researchers, Inc.; m.l. Sydney Byrd; m.r. Steve Vidler/Leo de Wys; t.l. Jerry Wachter/Leo de Wys. 26. l. R. C. Hermes/Photo Researchers, Inc.; r. Dan & Pat Valenti/DRK. 26–27: Scott Camaziine/Photo Researchers, Inc. **Unit 3** 38, 39: Ken Karp for MHSD. **Unit 4** 46: b GRP. 46–47: t. Ken Karp for MHSD. 50–51: Bill Waltzer for MHSD. 52: b.l., b.r., t.l. Jim Powell Studio for MHSD; t.r. Ken Karp for MHSD. 53: b.l., t.r. Jim Powell Studio for MHSD; b.r. Joseph Saches for MHSD. 55: b.l. Steve J. Sherman. 58: M. Dominguez/LG1 59: Nick Elgar/LGI. **Unit 5** 60–61: Bill Waltzer for MHSD. 64–65: Ken Karp for MHSD. **Unit 6** 80–81: Ken Karp for MHSD. 88–89: Elephant Records. **Celebrations** 101: *Wood Gatherer*, 1972, Oscar Howe, collection of Heidi Howe. © Adelaid Howe, 1983. 102–103: Ken Karp for MHSD. 108: Victor Englebert. 110: Ken Karp for MHSD. 111: Consolidated News Pictures, Benjamin E. Forte/Uniphoto. 113: Ken Karp for MHSD. **Music Library** 136: Ed Wheeler/Stock. 137: Bard Martin/New York Youth Symphony.

McGraw–Hill School Division thanks The Selmer Company, Inc., and its Ludwig/Musser Industries and Glaesel String Instrument Company subsidiaries for providing all instruments used in MHSD photographs in this music textbook series, with exceptions as follows. MHSD thanks Yamaha Corporation of America for French horn, euphonium, acoustic and electric guitars, soprano, alto, and bass recorders, piano, and vibraphone; MMB Music Inc., St. Louis, MO, for Studio 49 instruments; Rhythm Band Instruments, Fort Worth, TX, for resonator bells; Courtly Instruments, NY, for soprano and tenor recorder; Elderly Instruments, Lansing, MI, for autoharp, dulcimer, hammered dulcimer, mandolin, Celtic harp, whistles, and Andean flute.

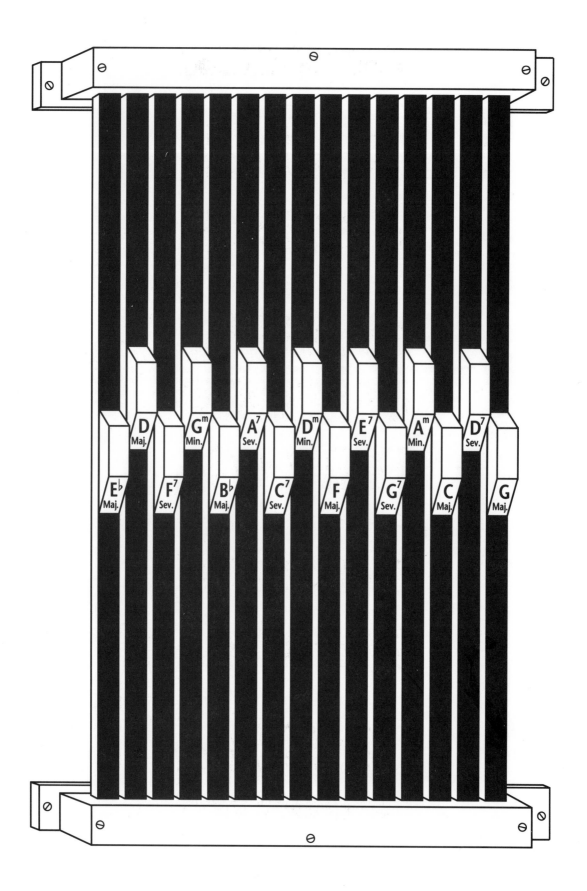